Stitch
with
One Line

33 Easy-to-Embroider
Minimalist Designs

Martina Unterfrauner
Nuray Hatun

SCHIFFER
CRAFT
4880 Lower Valley Road • Atglen, PA 19310

OTHER SCHIFFER CRAFT BOOKS ON RELATED SUBJECTS:

Sew for Yourself: 50 Great Garments from Recycled Fabric, Using 5 Basic Patterns,
Ingrid Bergtun & Ingrid Vik Lysne, ISBN 978-0-7643-6613-0

Juno's Nature Embroidery Notebook: Stitching Plants, Animals, and Stories, Juno, ISBN 978-0-7643-6422-8

Organic Embroidery, Meredith Woolnough, ISBN 978-0-7643-5613-1

Copyright © 2024 by Schiffer Publishing, Ltd.
Originally published as *One Line Drawings* © 2021 Christophorus Verlag, Munich. Translated from the German by Sharon Howe.

Photography by Elisabeth Berkau and Martina Unterfrauner except as otherwise noted.
Embroidery patterns by Merija Lina Melbarde and Martina Unterfrauner except as otherwise noted.

Additional photo and pattern credits: Shutterstock: p. 14 (porn-pawit), p. 14 (Singleline), p. 18 (Walnut Bird), p. 20 (Blinx), p. 22 (Walnut Bird), p. 28 (Keya), p. 30 (LivDeco), p. 32 (Walnut Bird), p. 35 (LivDeco), p. 40 (KNST ART STUDIO), p. 48 (ZenStockers), p. 56 (ShlyahovaYulia), p. 62 (DODOMO), p. 62 (san4ezz), p. 66 (abstract_art7), p. 64 (Aleona), p. 70 (i_am_Asya), p. 72 (Essl), p. 74 (Dasha D), p. 78 (LivDeco), p. 80 (valeriia63), p. 82 (LivDeco), p. 83 (Thamyris Salgueiro), 87 (ShotPrime Studio), p. 88 (Dasha D), p. 94 (Walnut Bird) p. 94 (jafara), p. 94 (Singleline), p. 94 (Pixel-Shot)

The authors thank these suppliers and sponsors: Butinette; Rico Design; Stoff und Stil; Freudenberg Performance Materials Apparel SE & Co.; Snaply; and Marabu.

Library of Congress Control Number: 2023940977

Designed by Martina Unterfrauner
Cover design by Ashley Millhouse
Type set in SaithikOpen Sans

ISBN: 978-0-7643-6758-8
Printed in China

Published by Schiffer Craft
An imprint of Schiffer Publishing, Ltd.
4880 Lower Valley Road
Atglen, PA 19310
Phone: (610) 593-1777; Fax: (610) 593-2002
Email: Info@schifferbooks.com
Web: www.schifferbooks.com

For our complete selection of fine books on this and related subjects, please visit our website at www.schifferbooks.com. You may also write for a free catalog.

Schiffer Publishing's titles are available at special discounts for bulk purchases for sales promotions or premiums. Special editions, including personalized covers, corporate imprints, and excerpts, can be created in large quantities for special needs. For more information, contact the publisher.

We are always looking for people to write books on new and related subjects. If you have an idea for a book, please contact us at proposals@schifferbooks.com.

CONTENTS

HOME

FASHION

DEAR EMBROIDERY FANS, CREATIVES, FASHIONISTAS . . .

Embroidery is a truly awesome art! Not just because of the beauty of the work itself, but also because of the dexterity, patience, and attention to detail of the embroiderer.

For a long time, embroidery suffered from a rather antiquated image. But in recent years all that has changed, and there are now plenty of excellent modern embroidery designs on the market. Not to mention all the exciting embroidery projects on the internet just waiting to be tried!

Why, though, do most projects still have to be done in miniature format, or give the impression of having been slaved over for weeks? That kind of approach no longer suits the lifestyle of creative working people. Surely there must be some great projects that are both quick and easy—and look fabulous too?

The answer to this question came in the shape of the "one-line" art that began to pop up on our Pinterest boards: stunning drawings that distill the essence of an object into just a few lines. We were instantly fascinated: here was something we could work with!

Before long, we had become embroidery junkies. We kept thinking of new ideas, new ways to showcase these lovely designs—and that's how this book was born. Our aim is to encourage experts and beginners alike to take up the needle. Because there is something remarkably meditative about embroidery. The only downside is that you'll never want to stop . . .

Happy embroidering!

Martina

Nuray

Basics

ONE-LINE DRAWINGS—WHAT MAKES THEM SO UNIQUE?

One-line drawings are all the rage. Yet, they're not a modern invention: the first ones date back to the early twentieth century and were made fashionable by no less than Pablo Picasso. He took a complex, realistic object and reduced it to a single continuous line (the horse pictured above was one of his first one-line drawings). Simple though it may look, anyone experimenting with this technique will soon realize how difficult it is to capture the "true essence" of an object in just one line.

There are many different ways of rendering one-line drawings: simple or complex, realistic or abstract, and with or without color elements. In this book, you'll also find projects featuring "open" one-line drawings, in which the line representing the design is left open in one or both directions and is thus infinitely extendable.

As you'll soon discover, there's a lot more to one-line art than meets the eye!

ONE-LINE DRAWINGS AS EMBROIDERY PATTERNS

You can find a wealth of drawings on all kinds of themes on the internet. This book focuses on animals, plants, and people. The patterns are chosen to reflect the wide range of possible shapes and stylistic techniques, and they're suitable for a variety of décor and fashion projects. Depending on type and style, some one-line drawings can be combined with others, used in series, or extended. The projects here are meant as a springboard to further designs, whether you base them on patterns from books or the internet, or perhaps even your own drawings!

When it comes to choosing an effective and workable drawing to embroider, size is key. For complex patterns in particular, it's best not to think too small.

Tip: Some of the designs in this book have been slightly modified for ease of embroidery, so that they appear as one line but are actually divided into two or three sections.

MATERIALS

Yarns

You can use almost any yarn for embroidery, as long as it doesn't distort your fabric. You'll soon discover which type of yarn works best. When choosing the right colors for your project, it is usually the case that less is more. The drawings work best against a strongly contrasting background. Below is an overview of the main types of yarn used in this book:

EMBROIDERY FLOSS

Floss is regarded as the classic embroidery fiber. It generally consists of six loosely twisted strands, so you can choose to work with one to six strands by pulling them gently to separate them. You'll find a whole range of embroidery floss on the market, including multicolored, metallic, and neon. Perle cotton is thicker and is used as a single strand.

CROCHET THREAD

This is a twisted cotton thread that keeps its shape in embroidery projects. It is suitable for most of the projects in this book. It should be used with a needle size of 1.5 to 2.25.

YARN

Crewel yarn, also called tapestry wool, is used for embroidery and needlepoint. You can also use ordinary yarn, which has the advantage of being cheap and available in a wide range of thicknesses and colors. When embroidering washable fabrics, always check to make sure the yarn is compatible with the fabric-washing instructions.

SEWING THREAD

This is available in a variety of thicknesses and is suitable for fine hand embroidery and machine embroidery alike (see "Machine Embroidery," p. 15). The thickest and strongest include denim and buttonhole threads.

Fabrics and More

You can embroider more or less any fabric. The most suitable are woven fabrics with a smooth surface, such as cotton or linen, although wool and felt are also excellent. Knit and stretchy fabrics are a bit trickier, but even they are no problem, given the right material and technique. Before embroidering store-bought textiles and garments, always make sure the material is suitable for your planned project—and remember to wash it first!

In this book, we also suggest various alternative substrates such as paper fabric (like Kraft-tex or SnapPap), cork, and wood. It's always worth experimenting!

Tool Kit

Fusible interfacing: A material with a heat-activated adhesive coating on one side, which is ironed onto fabric or paper. Fine fabrics in particular should be stabilized in this way prior to embroidering, to prevent them from puckering (use the lightest type of interfacing for them). Elastic interfacings are also available for stretchy fabrics such as jersey. Follow the manufacturer's instructions; usually you place the adhesive side down on the wrong side of your fabric and cover it with a damp cloth, then iron on for about fifteen seconds, a section at a time.

Needles: There are countless varieties of embroidery needles, so you need to make sure you have the right one for your yarn and substrate. Your best bet is to buy a set of different-sized needles and try them out.

Embroidery hoops: These keep the fabric taut while you work. Though not a must, they are helpful for some embroidery projects. To insert the fabric, pull the two rings apart and place the fabric on the inner ring so that the design is well centered. Then place the outer ring on top and press down.

Pins: For holding the design in place on fabric, paper, or stabilizer. Keep these handy at all times!

Embroidery scissors: Very small, sharp scissors for cutting off threads: an essential tool.

Fabric scissors: Another essential, specially designed for cutting fabric.

Double-sided adhesive fusible bonding web or tape: Comes with a pressure-sensitive adhesive on each side to temporarily hold both materials in place before you fuse.

SCALING

All the designs for the projects are supplied at the back of the book. Some are at the exact size used in a project and can be traced directly from the page where they appear. To adapt the size of a design, you can use any of the following:

Photocopier: A quick and easy way of scaling designs is to use a conventional photocopier with a manual scaling function. A scale factor below 100% will reduce the design; a value above 100% will enlarge it. You may need to do a bit of experimenting until you get the right size.

Printer: If you have a printer at home, you can photograph or scan the design first to size it, then print it out.

Screen/monitor: If you have a computer but no printer, you can photograph the design and copy it from the screen. To do this, open the photo on the screen and adjust the design to the required size, using the zoom function. Now copy it onto paper (see "Light Box Method," p. 9). If you want your design to be larger than the screen, you will need to copy it in sections by moving the screen view and continuing where you left off each time. Make sure you keep the same zoom factor throughout.

TRANSFER METHODS

There are many ways of transferring the design to the fabric, and choosing the right one can be essential to the success of your project. We've therefore provided a recommendation with each set of instructions, although this will of course depend on which substrate you are using. The following methods worked well for the projects in this book:

LIGHT BOX METHOD

With this method, a window pane (or computer monitor) is used as a light box (assuming most people are unlikely to have one at home). It is only suitable for pale and relatively thin fabrics though.

Method: Attach the paper containing the design to the window or monitor with adhesive tape. Place the fabric over the design right side out (the side you want to embroider) and pin it to the paper. Now trace the design with a suitable pen (see "Fabric Markers" below) and unpin the fabric again.

WATER-SOLUBLE STABILIZER

This is suitable for all washable fabrics, especially thin ones, and has the added advantage of stiffening your fabric while you embroider. Afterward, you can simply wash it out. You can also buy self-adhesive stabilizer, which prevents the design from slipping as you work. This dissolves when soaked in water, allowing easy removal. It is ideal for embroidering jersey shirts.

Method: Transfer the design to the stabilizer and cut out generously around it, then pin or stick it to your fabric. Once you've finished embroidering, trim away the excess stabilizer and leave to soak in water for at least an hour. (If using a self-adhesive stabilizer, peel it off carefully.) Finally, rinse off under running water.

TEAR-AWAY STABILIZERS

This transfer method is particularly suitable for dark and deep-pile fabrics, but also for all other textiles. It has the advantage of stiffening the fabric while you work so that it doesn't get pulled out of shape.

Method: Place the pattern under the stabilizer and trace with a pen. Cut out generously around the design and position it on your fabric. Pin in place, then embroider the design directly onto the stabilizer. Finally, remove all the pins and tear away the outer edges of the stabilizer from around the design. Then carefully tease out the inner remnants. A (blunt) needle is handy for this.

TRANSFER PAPER

This is used to trace the design onto the fabric. It is available in different colors, making it suitable for any light or dark fabric with a smooth surface (carbon paper is another good alternative). Bear in mind, though, that this will leave permanent lines, which your embroidery will need to cover.

Method: Place the transfer paper between the design and fabric and trace the lines with a pen, pressing down hard. The thinner the pen, the thinner the visible line on your fabric will be.

FABRIC MARKERS

There are all kinds of tools for drawing on and marking fabric. In addition to the classic tailor's chalk, the following markers are recommended:

IRON-OFF MARKERS:	Heat-erasable—lines disappear when ironed.
SELF-ERASING MARKERS:	Lines disappear on their own over time—therefore suitable only for quickly completed projects.
WATER-SOLUBLE FELT-TIP PENS:	Lines disappear on contact with water.

WEAVING IN & SECURING THE THREAD

Whichever embroidery stitch you opt for, you want to make sure it can't come undone and is worked in neatly at the back. There are various methods of securing your thread:

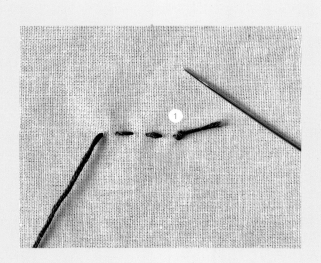

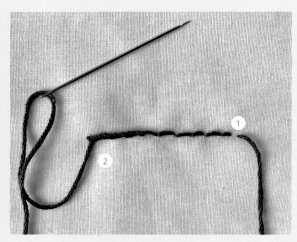

METHOD 1: KNOTTING

The simplest way is to make a knot at the back. ① The trouble with this method is that the knot can slip through coarse fabrics or leave an unsightly bump. It is also unsuitable for washable fabrics and textiles, where the knot may work loose. On the other hand, it's ideal for materials such as paper or wood.

METHOD 2: WEAVING IN

The weaving-in method is used mainly for securing the thread end, but is also suitable for changing color or introducing a new piece of yarn.

How to do it: First, thread your needle and bring it up through the fabric from the back, leaving an approx. 2" (5 cm) tail of yarn behind. ①
Hold this with one hand while you sew the first stitch, then continue embroidering normally.
When you get to the end, leave another tail and weave in both threads at the back. To do this, thread the needle and pass it under four or five existing stitches in one direction, then repeat in the other direction (see instructions for whipped backstitch, p. 11). ②

TIP

Ideally, the thread length should be no longer than the distance from your fingertip to your elbow; otherwise your threads can easily become tangled or frayed as you work.

BASIC STITCHES

One-line designs are embroidered using simple line stitches.
Most projects in this book can be done with any of the stitches below.

Crochet thread   *Embroidery floss*   *Yarn*

BACKSTITCH

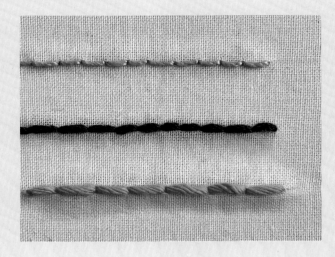

Backstitch is the basis of all line stitches and is ideal for most projects. The stitches overlap on the reverse, resembling *stem stitch* (p. 12).

How to do it: Bring your needle up through the fabric from back to front and insert it one stitch length down the line. Move on two stitch lengths and bring it back up again. Then move back one stitch length, insert the needle, and come up again after two stitch lengths, and so on.

WHIPPED BACKSTITCH

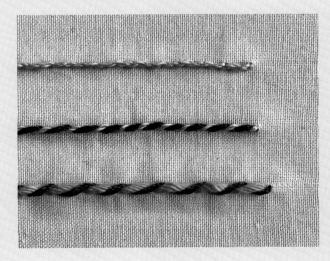

This stitch is based on the *backstitch* and looks almost like a pen-drawn line. Depending on the desired effect, the stitches can be "whipped" (wrapped) with a yarn of the same or different color and thickness.

How to do it: Embroider the whole line, using *backstitch*. When you get to the end, bring the needle up through the fabric from back to front. Now work your way back along the line, passing the needle under each stitch from the same side to ensure even whipping. Keep going until you reach the end.

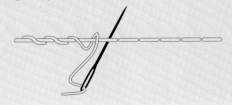

STEM STITCH

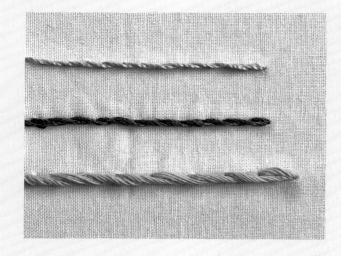

This stitch looks like a twisted cord. You need to keep your stitches very even for this one and make them smaller on curves (curved designs can be a little more challenging!) On the reverse, this looks like *backstitch* (p. 11).

How to do it: Bring the needle up through the fabric from back to front, insert it after the desired stitch length, and pull the thread back through. Move back half a stitch length and come up again just beside your last stitch. Always keep your working thread below the line of stitching.

SPLIT STITCH

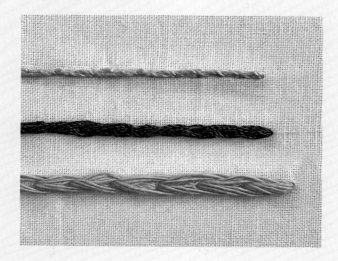

Split stitch is rather similar to chain stitch, depending on the type of yarn you are using. It is best done with multistrand or twisted thread. On the reverse, it looks like *backstitch* (p. 11).

How to do it: Bring the needle up through the fabric from back to front, insert it after the desired stitch length, and pull the thread back through. Come up again halfway along the stitch, poking the needle through the thread as centrally as possible so that it "splits" into two halves.

CHAIN STITCH

This looped stitch creates thick outlines. On the reverse, it looks like *backstitch* (p. 11).

How to do it: Bring the needle up through the fabric from back to front, insert it close to where you came up, and bring it up again a stitch length down the line. Then pass the thread around the tip of the needle and pull gently into a loop. Pull out the needle and repeat the previous steps.
To finish, insert the needle exactly in front of the last loop and pull the thread through to the back.

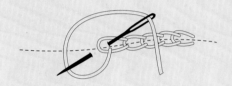

PICK STITCH

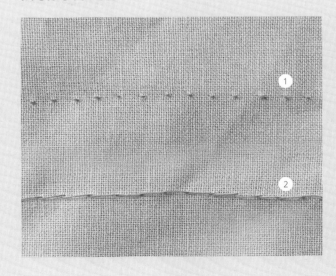

In this book, pick stitch is used exclusively for appliquéing cords. On the right side, you end up with just a dotted line. ① If the yarn is the same color as the background, it will be almost invisible. On the wrong side, you will get an overlapping effect. ②

How to do it: Pick stitch is based on the same principle as *backstitch* (p. 11). This time the needle is not inserted right next to where you came up, however, but very slightly to the left of it.

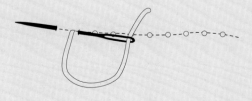

"HUMMINGBIRD" TOP

Transfer and embroidery:
See "Machine Embroidery," p. 15

MACHINE EMBROIDERY

One-line drawings lend themselves really well to embroidering by machine. "Freehand embroidery" can be done on just about any sewing machine. The technique may feel a bit unfamiliar at first, but once you get the hang of it, you'll find it quick, straightforward, and great fun!

1. Preparing the Machine

First mount the embroidery foot. Then select the following settings:
- Stitch length: 0
- Stitch type: straight
- Thread tension: medium

Now lower the feed dogs so that the fabric can be guided by hand instead of automatically. (Some machines also have a needle plate—a small piece of plastic that covers the feed dogs.)

2. Sewing Thread

The thickness of the sewing thread makes a huge difference to the look of your embroidery. A thin thread will produce very fine lines that get thicker the more times you go over them. This results in a scribble effect (see "Hummingbird Top," p. 14). For simple stitching, it is best to use a very thick thread (e.g., denim). For the bobbin, always use normal sewing thread.

3. Transferring the Design

See also "Transfer Methods" (p. 9).

Tip: If using *tear-away stabilizer* to transfer your design, you will need to remove it after the first line of stitching. You can then go over your line again as many times as you wish. (If you wait till afterward, you will struggle to remove the bits of stabilizer from between the lines.)

If you want to stiffen your fabric permanently with a fusible interfacing (see "Tool Kit," p. 8), you can transfer the design at the same time. To do this, draw the design in reverse on the interfacing and iron it onto the wrong side of the fabric. Now stitch along the line on this side. Finally, turn the fabric the right way around and go over the line as many times as you wish.

4. Preparing the Fabric

The fabric should be stretched as taut as possible for embroidering. You may find an *embroidery hoop* (see "Tool Kit," p. 8) useful for smaller designs. Thinner or stretchy fabrics should always be stabilized with a special fusible interfacing before embroidering (see "Tool Kit," p. 8).

5. And Off You Go!

Now lift the embroidery foot and place the fabric underneath. Unlike in normal sewing, the fabric/embroidery hoop is guided by hand instead of by the feed dogs. To get a feel for freehand embroidery, it's worth doing a bit of "doodling" first.

Depending on the desired effect, you can now embroider the drawing as a single, precise line or machine over it multiple times.

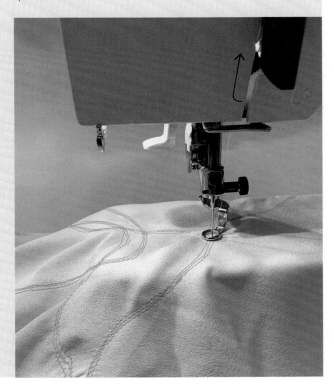

"TOUCH" PILLOW

Transfer method: Transfer paper (p. 9)
Embroidery: Stem stitch (p. 12)

Home

Whether on cushions, storage containers, or vases—
one-line drawings are an homage to art and the home.

(See page 95 for the patterns for these projects.)

VELVET CUSHION
Eucalyptus

Cushions make the home cozy and create ambience. In combination with velvet, this filigree drawing lends an instant touch of elegance to any interior. When it comes to the choice of cushion, bear in mind that short-pile fabrics such as velveteen or upholstery velvet are easier to embroider than ordinary cotton velvet. This design also makes a lovely picture to hang on the wall (see "A Few More Ideas," p. 94).

MATERIALS

- Cushion cover with cushion. Used here: 21.5" × 21.5" (55 × 55 cm), velveteen.
- Suitable transfer medium (e.g., tear-away stabilizer)
- Yarn (e.g., cream crochet thread)
- Embroidery needle

1. Transfer: *Tear-away stabilizer* (p. 9) is best for pile fabrics such as velveteen or velvet. Copy the design to the stabilizer, cut it out roughly, and pin it to the cushion cover.

2. Embroidery: Starting from the stem, embroider along the line (e.g., using a small *split stitch* [p. 12]). *Whipped backstitch* (p. 11) is also well suited to this delicate design. Finally, remove the stabilizer carefully with a blunt needle.

CORK PICTURE
Panda

MATERIALS

- Picture frame with mat. Used here: image size 9.5" × 9.5" (24 × 24 cm).
- Corkboard
- White acrylic paint
- Paintbrush
- Masking tape
- Suitable transfer medium (e.g., tear-away stabilizer)
- Yarn (e.g., black crochet thread)
- Embroidery needle
- Double-sided adhesive tape

This timeless Asian-style image looks good in any setting and works well in combination with other designs. Beyond its aesthetic appeal, the panda also symbolizes strength and protection and is much prized in China as a national emblem. It is particularly effective against the cork background, which is great for embroidering—whether by hand or machine.

The panda also makes an attractive addition to clothing and accessories (see "A Few More Ideas," p. 94).

PANDA CORK PICTURE

1. Prep: Cut the corkboard to the size of your picture frame and divide it in half diagonally with a piece of masking tape.

2. Color design: Coat one-half with acrylic paint and leave to dry thoroughly.

3. Transfer: The best way to transfer the design is with *tear-away stabilizer* (p. 9). Now center the design and pin in place.

4. Embroidery: *Whipped backstitch* (p. 11) works very well for this intricate drawing. Instead of weaving in the beginning and end threads, secure them with small knots to keep the picture nice and flat.

5. Mounting: Attach your finished work to the back panel of the frame with double-sided adhesive tape and insert into the frame together with the mat. (Do not cover with glass.)

MORE ASIAN INSPIRATION . . .

TABLE LINENS
Ginkgo

NAPKINS

1. Color design: Draw a circle in one corner of the napkin. Ours is 1.5" (3.5 cm) dia. Color it in with fabric paint. Leave to dry thoroughly.

2. Transfer: Transfer the smaller of the two designs from the pattern to the fabric, using *transfer paper* (p. 9).

3. Embroidery: Remove one strand from the embroidery floss and embroider along the line, using a small *backstitch* (p. 11).

TABLECLOTH

1. Transfer: Scale the larger of the two designs to two further sizes (see "Scaling," p. 8). Transfer to *water-soluble stabilizer* (p. 9) and cut out roughly. Arrange in a pattern on the tablecloth and attach in place.

2. Embroidery: Adjust the machine to the required settings and stitch along the lines (see "Machine Embroidery," p. 15). Soak in water to remove the stabilizer.

MATERIALS

For the napkins:
- Plain fabric napkins
- Gold fabric paint
- Paintbrush
- Suitable transfer medium (e.g., transfer paper)
- Yarn (e.g., black embroidery floss)
- Embroidery needle

For the tablecloth:
- Plain fabric tablecloth
- Suitable transfer medium (e.g., water-soluble stabilizer)
- Sewing thread (e.g., white denim thread)
- Sewing machine with embroidery foot

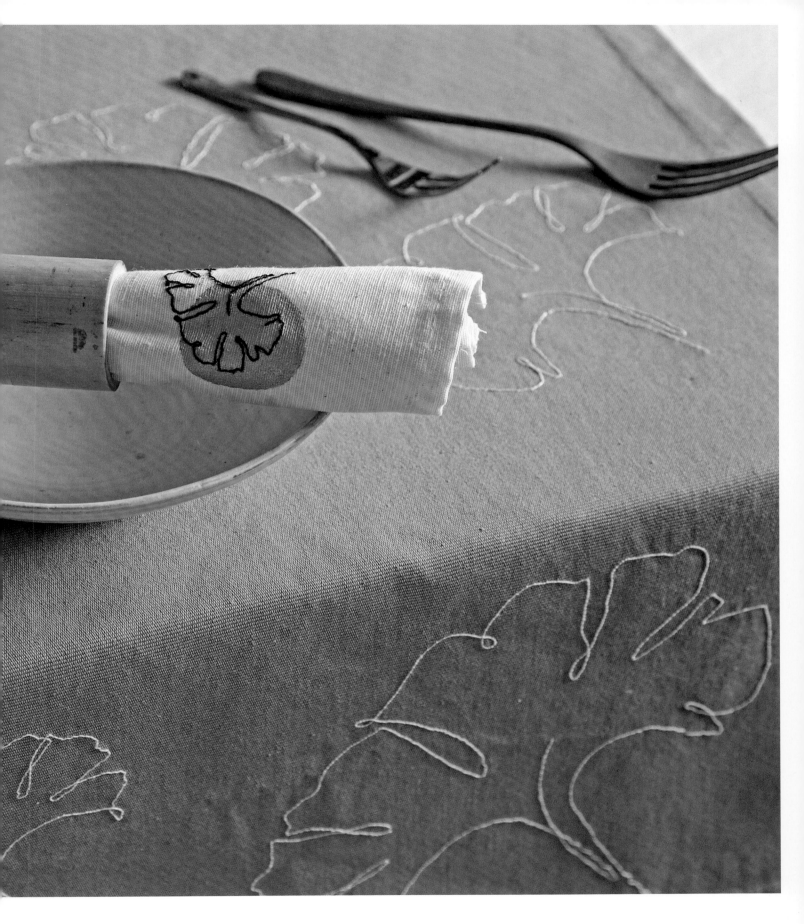

PICTURE
Shy Lady

MATERIALS

- Picture frame with mat. Image size used here: 15.75" × 19.5" (40 × 50 cm).
- Paper fabric (like Kraft-tex or SnapPap)
- Acrylic paint in various colors
- Flat-bristle brush
- Utility knife and ruler
- Adhesive masking tape
- Pencil
- Transfer paper
- Yarn (e.g., gray embroidery floss, slightly thicker than your needle)
- Pins
- Double-sided adhesive tape

Color elements can really enhance a one-line drawing. This picture uses a special type of paper as a substrate: Paper fabric is tear resistant and suitable for painting and embroidering, which makes it ideal for mixed media. Embroidering on paper is easy to do, provided you follow a few basic rules.

PICTURE

1. Prep: Cut the paper fabric to the size of your frame with the utility knife, then stick it to your work surface with adhesive masking tape (paper fabric is very resilient).

2. Color design: To arrange the color areas to best effect, you first need to decide on the position of your design. Transfer the outlines roughly with a pencil and sketch in the color blocks. Then erase the pencil lines so they won't show through the color later on. Fill in the blocks with (diluted) acrylic paint, starting with the palest one. Leave to dry thoroughly.

3. Transfer: This project works well with *transfer paper* (p. 9). You need to keep your lines very fine, though, so that they will be covered by your embroidery later on.   1

Alternatively, place the design directly on the substrate and make prepunched holes with the needle as described in step 4.

4. Prepunching: Punch holes very carefully at evenly spaced intervals. On narrow curves, make the holes closer together.   2

5. Embroidery: Begin by securing your thread with a small knot.   3   Alternatively, you can stick it down on the reverse with adhesive tape. (Avoid weaving in so as to keep the picture nice and flat.)

Embroider your design, using *backstitch* (p. 11).   4 (The holes should no longer be visible. If they are, just use a slightly thicker yarn.)

Alternatively, a *whipped backstitch* in the same color yarn will also work well.

6. Mounting: Attach your finished picture to the back panel of the frame, using double-sided adhesive tape, and insert into the wooden frame together with the mat. (Do not cover with glass.)

TIP

Instead of paper fabric, you can also use other types of paper such as cardstock, canvas, or watercolor paper. As a general rule, stiffer paper is better, although thinner types can also be used with a *fusible interfacing* (see "Tool Kit," p. 8). Simply place the interfacing on the reverse side of the paper and iron all over.

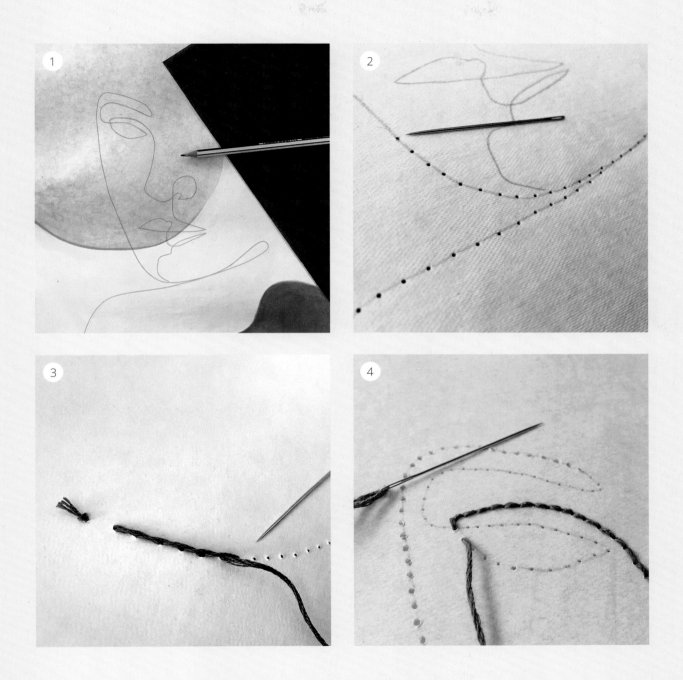

LAMPSHADE
Butterfly

This butterfly design is open on both sides, making it ideal for wraparound embroidery, as in the case of this lampshade. The line can be modified or extended as you wish.

When embroidering lampshades, the secret is to keep the reverse side as neat and knot-free as possible, bearing in mind that your stitching will show through later on.

MATERIALS

- Plain lampshade. Used here: 5.5" (14 cm) dia.
- Tear-away stabilizer
- Yarn (e.g., black crochet thread)
- Embroidery needle

1. Prep: Cut the *tear-away stabilizer* (p. 9) to the height and circumference of the lampshade, allowing an extra 1.5" (4 cm) on the narrow side of the rectangle.

2. Transfer: Decide where to position the design on the lampshade, and mark the spot on the stabilizer. Wrap the stabilizer around the lamp and pin the ends together at the center back. Extend the lines leading away from the butterfly in either direction so that they curve attractively around the lampshade and meet at the center back.

3. Embroidery: Embroider the design using *whipped backstitch* (p. 11). Start at the center back and secure the end of the thread with a small knot. Punch a hole with the needle before each stitch and embroider in the usual way (see "Picture" instructions, p. 26, step 4), finishing at the center back where you started. Secure the end of the thread with a knot.

DISPLAY CARDS
Flowers

These hand-embroidered fabric cards make a lovely gift for special occasions—or a stylish decoration for the home. The colored vases painted onto the card add another dimension to the simple elegance of the flower designs. These designs also look great on clothing (see "Rose Sweater," p. 60).

MATERIALS

- Cardstock for reverse side and mat
- Utility knife
- Smooth woven fabric
- Fabric or acrylic paints
- Fine-bristle brush
- Double-sided adhesive fusible bonding web
- Suitable transfer medium (e.g., iron-off marker)
- Thin yarn (e.g., rose-pink buttonhole thread)
- Embroidery needle
- Embroidery hoop (optional)
- Spray adhesive

1. Prep: Cut two rectangles measuring 9" (23 cm) h × 6" (15 cm) w out of the cardstock. Now take one of the rectangles and trim it to make the mat.

2. Transfer: Copy the design onto the fabric. The *light box method* (p. 9) works well with pale colors. (If you are using an embroidery hoop, be sure to leave enough space around the edges.)

3. Color design: Paint on your own vase shapes, using fabric paint, and leave to dry thoroughly. Draw in the flower stems again if necessary.

4. Embroidery: Insert your fabric in the embroidery hoop if using (see "Tool Kit," p. 8). The stitching should be as flat as possible on the reverse, and as neat and knot-free as possible. *Stem stitch* (p. 12) is very good for this, for example.

5. Mounting: Trim your finished work so that it is slightly smaller than the prepared cardstock, and iron it on with *double-sided adhesive fusible bonding web* (see "Tool Kit," p. 8). Glue on the mat with spray adhesive.

COSMETIC BAG
Palm Leaf

MATERIALS

- Plain fabric purse. Used here: 11" (28 cm) w × 7" (18 cm) h.
- Optionally for DIY version: cotton fabric, zip fastener (12" [30 cm] long), and sewing machine
- Fabric marker (e.g., chalk)
- White and gold fabric paints
- Fine-bristle brush
- Suitable transfer medium (e.g., transfer paper)
- Yarn (e.g., gray embroidery floss)
- Embroidery needle

One-line drawings of tropical foliage like this palm leaf look great combined with a splash of color, and work well on both fabric and paper. If using a purchased purse, make sure it doesn't have an inside lining or pockets. Alternatively, you can make your own in no time, giving you complete creative freedom! Instructions for making a quick and easy version can be found on the next page.

COSMETIC BAG

1. Cutting (optional)**:** Cut two rectangles measuring 12" (30 cm) w × 8" (20 cm) h out of the fabric.

2. Making the bag (optional)**:** Neaten the edges of both rectangles all the way around, using zigzag stitch. Press the top 0.5" (1 cm) of the fabric edges under with the iron. Now place the pressed edges of both pieces alongside the zipper and stitch in place with the sewing machine.

Open the zipper halfway and place the fabric pieces right sides together (with the outer material facing in). Stitch the side and bottom seams all the way around, leaving a 0.5" (1 cm) seam allowance.

3. Color design: Draw in the color areas on the right side with a fabric marker. Color in the white area, then the gold one, with fabric paint. Leave to dry thoroughly, then set with the iron.

4. Transfer: Copy the design onto the fabric (e.g., using *transfer paper* [p. 9]).

5. Embroidery: Embroider along the line, using *whipped backstitch* (p. 11) or another line stitch of your choice. In this case, the line of backstitch was sewn first, using three threads from the embroidery floss, then whipped with the remaining threads.

MATERIALS

- Plain fabric bag. Used here: 4" (10 cm) w × 4.75" (12 cm).
- Suitable transfer medium (e.g., transfer paper)
- Yarn (e.g., pink, yellow, and green embroidery floss)
- Embroidery needle

MORE TROPICAL FLAIR . . .

SOAP BAG
Flamingo

1. Transfer: Copy the designs onto the bag (e.g., using *transfer paper* [p. 9]).

2. Embroidery: Embroider along the lines in *whipped backstitch* (p. 11), using just one to three threads from the embroidery floss. First embroider the flamingo in pink backstitch, then whip your stitches with yellow yarn. Embroider the leaves in plain green. In this case, the embroidery floss was whipped with a single thread.

TIP

You can also make your own bag with very little effort. That way you can embroider the fabric before sewing it together, which makes the job easier.

WOODEN TRINKET BOX *Feather*

MATERIALS

- Plywood box. Used here: 6" (15 cm) w × 4" (10 cm) h.
- Parchment paper and pen
- Pushpin
- Cordless drill with wood bit. Used here: approx. 0.05" (1.5 mm) dia.
- Sandpaper (optional)
- Masking tape
- Acrylic paint
- Paintbrush
- Yarn (e.g., cream crochet thread)
- Embroidery needle (slightly thinner than the prepunched holes)

You can never have enough trinket boxes for jewelry and all your little treasures—especially when they're as decorative as this one! With this project, preparation is key. The holes must be just the right size for the needle and yarn and need to be drilled with great care and precision: once made, there's no going back! For that reason, it's a good idea to practice on a piece of plywood first.

WOODEN TRINKET BOX

1. Transfer: Copy the design to the box with a pencil. The best way to do this is to trace the drawing in reverse onto parchment paper, using a (soft) pencil, then place the paper on the box with the design facedown and go over the outline with your pencil. Alternatively, you can use transfer paper—but remember the lines will be permanent!

2. Preparing the holes: Using the pushpin, make a small indentation in the wood approx. every 0.15" (4 mm) to prevent the drill bit from slipping. 1 Shorten the intervals on curved sections so as to avoid an angular effect, but don't make the holes too close together.

3. Drilling the holes: Now drill the holes with the wood bit. 2 They should be just large enough for the threaded needle to pass through. Smooth away any splinters with sandpaper and erase the pencil lines.

4. Color design: Place a strip of masking tape diagonally across the lid of the box and coat one-half with acrylic paint. Leave to dry thoroughly. If any of the holes get blocked with paint, you can easily unblock them with the pushpin once dry.

5. Embroidery: Secure the beginning of the thread with a knot on the inside of the lid. Now embroider through the holes, using *backstitch* (p. 11). 3 Finally, secure the end of the thread with another knot.

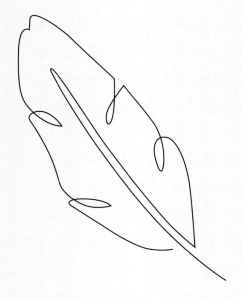

TIP

Even thicker wood can be embroidered using this method—just make the diameter of the predrilled holes slightly larger and use thicker yarn or a cord.

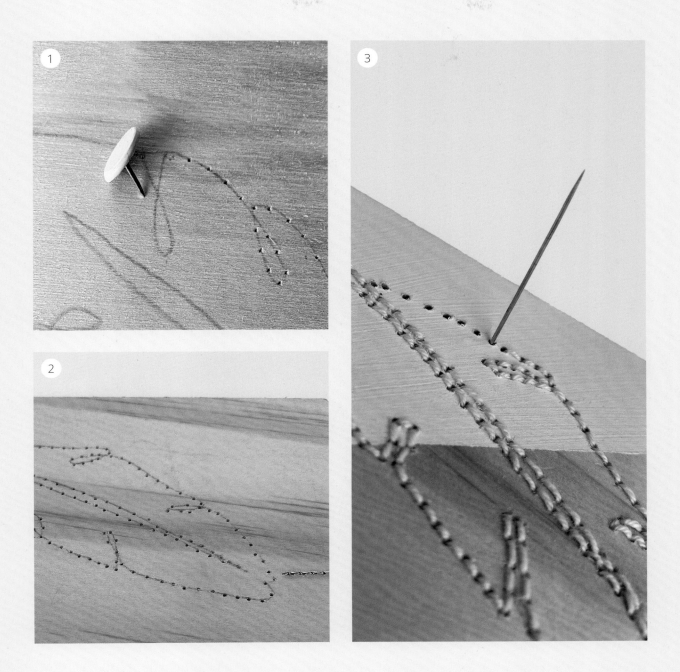

WALL ART
Girl with a Bun

This charmingly childlike drawing can be used to create a whole series of framed embroidered faces complete with hair. A decorative highlight for the kids' room—or your own!

MATERIALS

- Wooden embroidery hoop. Used here: 5" (13 cm) dia.
- Woven fabric (e.g., linen)
- Suitable transfer medium (e.g., transfer paper)
- Yarn (e.g., black and pink embroidery floss)
- Embroidery needle
- Black yarn for bun
- Chopsticks
- Craft glue
- Sewing needle and thread

1. Transfer: First copy the design to the fabric (e.g., with *transfer paper* [p. 9]). Leave enough space around it for the embroidery hoop.

2. Prep: Cut the fabric to size. Center the hoop on the reverse side of the design and draw a circle around it with a radius of approx. 2.75" (7 cm). Cut out and insert the fabric in the hoop, making sure it is stretched taut (the screw thread should be at the top).

3. Embroidery: *Backstitch* (p. 11) is well suited to the childlike quality of this drawing. For the cheek, embroider a spiral in pink yarn, working from the outside in.

4. Mounting: Wind the yarn around the screw thread of the hoop to make a bun. First, tie the yarn around the center of the screw, then start winding in a figure of eight. After the first few times, insert the chopsticks and continue winding until you end up with a little ball of yarn. Secure the end with craft glue. Finally, gather in the overhanging fabric at the back with large stitches so that it lies flat.

ANIMAL PILLOW
Foxy

MATERIALS

- Fabric for front panel. Used here: dusty-green linen, approx. 23.5" (60 cm) w × 26" (66 cm) h.
- Fabric for back panel, dimensions same as for front (e.g., cream-colored cotton)
- Fabric marker (e.g., chalk)
- Suitable transfer medium (e.g., transfer paper)
- Yarn (e.g., white wool)
- Embroidery needle
- Sewing machine and sewing thread
- Fiber fill

This cuddly critter looks great on a homemade pillow and is really quick and easy to create. If you use cotton, it will be easily washable as a snuggly friend for children. And instead of the fox, you can also pick a favorite animal to immortalize in your one-line design. You'll find other suitable animal patterns in this book.

PILLOW

1. Transfer: Copy the design to the linen fabric (e.g., with *transfer paper* [p. 9]). Be sure to leave enough space around it to cut out your cushion.

2. Embroidery: Embroider the design with yarn. We have used *split stitch* (p. 12) here, but you can use any line stitch you like.

3. Cutting: Draw a nice silhouette around your finished design and cut out, leaving a 0.5" (1 cm) seam allowance.

Now cut out a matching piece from the cotton fabric. For this, place the front panel on the cotton fabric so that both outer sides are facing in. Copy the outline onto the fabric and cut out.

4. Sewing: Machine the two pieces of fabric together all the way around, leaving an approx. 4" (10 cm) opening at the bottom. Take your scissors and make a vertical cut on either side of the opening to just before the seam. Now trim the seam allowances (up to the opening) by 0.25" (0.5 cm) all the way around and finish with a narrow zigzag stitch. Press the seam allowances open with the iron and turn the cushion onto the right side. Fill with fiber fill (don't overstuff!). Finally, sew up the opening by using a small *pick stitch* (p. 13).

MORE CREATURE COMFORTS FOR THE HOME . . .

CANVAS BASKET
Bunny

1. Color design: Cut two circles out of a piece of fabric and pin them to the basket so that they overlap. If necessary, trim away the overlap to ensure a smooth, flat surface. Sew the circles onto the basket, using *pick stitch* (p. 13).

2. Transfer: Copy the drawing onto *tear-away stabilizer* (p. 9), cut out roughly, and pin to the basket.

3. Embroidery: Embroider the design using *split stitch* (p. 12) or another line stitch of your choice. Keep the thread relatively taut as you work. Finally, remove the stabilizer carefully with a blunt needle.

MATERIALS

- Plain canvas basket. Used here: 11.5" (29 cm) dia., 9.75" (25 cm) h.
- Fluffy material (e.g., white and pink felt)
- Suitable transfer medium (e.g., tear-away stabilizer)
- Yarn (e.g., gray embroidery floss)
- Embroidery needle

TIP

For an attractive variation on the color design, try appliquéing wool roving, using a felting needle.

DISH TOWELS
Hummingbirds

With open one-line drawings, you can produce seamless patterns by joining designs together. This one is a symbiosis of hummingbird and lily—two originally separate drawings (pp. 14 and 30).

MATERIALS

- Woven fabric. Used here: cotton in mustard and mint green, 14.5" (37 cm) w × 10.75" (27.5 cm) h.
- Suitable transfer medium (e.g., water-soluble stabilizer)
- Sewing machine with embroidery foot
- Yarn for upper thread (e.g., denim thread in black and mustard)
- Sewing yarn for bobbin thread (in matching colors)
- Optional: embroidery needle and yarn for decorative stitching (e.g., crochet thread in beige and white)

1. Cutting: Draw a rectangle on the fabric in the specified dimensions. (These are for three rows of four hummingbirds and can be extended as required.) Mark a seam allowance of 0.5" (1 cm) all the way around and cut out. Now cut out an identical rectangle from the stabilizer.

2. Transfer: Arrange the design into a continuous pattern. To do this, first trace it (including the border) from the pattern pages and cut it out. Then copy the shape onto the stabilizer, moving it along a step at a time as shown in the layout diagram on p. 96.

3. Embroidery: Pin the stabilizer to the fabric and machine along the lines on the appropriate setting (see "Machine Embroidery," p. 15). Dissolve the stabilizer in water.

4. Finishing: Once it's completed, neaten the edges of the fabric, press under, and topstitch to finish. Alternatively, embroider the edges with a decorative stitch of your choice.

VASE
Naive Art

There are plenty of exquisitely painted vases, lanterns, and other vessels with a one-line design—but how do you get the same effect with embroidery? Easy: you simply embroider your fabric and glue it on! Just be sure to choose a straight-sided vessel so you don't end up with any wrinkles.

MATERIALS

- Smooth woven fabric (e.g., cream-colored cotton)
- Straight glass vase. Used here: 6" (15 cm) dia., 12" (30 cm) h.
- Suitable transfer medium (e.g., iron-off marker)
- Embroidery yarn (e.g., crochet thread in blue, yellow, and pink)
- Embroidery needle
- Decoupage medium
- Parchment paper
- Small sponge or soft cotton cloth

1. Prep: Cut a rectangle out of the fabric in the same dimensions as the vase, allowing an extra 0.75"–1" (2–3 cm) in length so that the two ends will overlap at the center back when glued in place. It is best to cut out the rectangle 0.25" (1 cm) larger all around to begin with. You can then trim it to the final dimensions once you've finished embroidering: this will stop the edges from fraying.

2. Transfer: Copy the design to the fabric, using the *light box method* (p. 9), for example.

3. Embroidery: *Backstitch* (p. 11) lends itself well to the style of this drawing. **Tip:** With backstitch, your stitches will overlap on the reverse. This means you will need to use a relatively fine thread to prevent them from showing through. (With split, chain, or stem stitch, the reverse remains virtually flat.) Keep your stitching very neat on this side and always use knots to secure the ends of the yarn.

4. Finishing: Trim off the excess from the long sides of your finished piece. Place the fabric reverse side up on the parchment paper. Apply Paperpatch glue quickly and wrap around your vase, taking care to avoid any creases or bubbles.

CUSHION
Eye-Catcher

MATERIALS

- Cushion cover with cushion. Used here: 15.75" × 15.75" (40 × 40 cm).
- Suitable transfer medium (e.g., transfer paper)
- White cotton or synthetic cord (approx. 0.15" [4 mm] dia.)
- Fabric glue pen (e.g., Sewline)
- Sewing needle and thread (in same color as cord)

Here, the thick, three-dimensional outline reinforces the effect of the minimalist design. Instead of conventional embroidery techniques, it is achieved by appliquéing a cord along the line. This quick, straightforward method is ideal for simple one-line drawings and lettering—not just on cushions, but on bags and T-shirts too (see "Wildcat Sweatshirt," p. 80).

CUSHION

1. Transfer: Copy the design to the cushion cover (e.g., with *transfer paper* [p. 9]). Don't worry about the lines—they will be covered by the cord.

2. Prep: Cut a long piece of cord to the required size or, alternatively, work straight from the reel. Once cut, cotton cords fray relatively easily, so you will need to seal the end first: a drop of transparent craft glue will do the job. 1a Synthetic cords can be permanently sealed using a lighter: just singe the end briefly to fuse the fibers together. 1b

3. Laying the cord: Lay a section of cord along the line of the design and attach to the fabric, using the fabric glue pen. 2

Tip: You can also use double-sided fabric tape for this. Be careful not to sew directly over the taped area later on, however, in case the tape gets stuck to the needle. Continue step by step until the entire design is laid and fixed in place. It is important to make sure the cord lies flat and is not stretched too taut.

Finally, seal the other end of the cord with the lighter or glue.

4. Appliqué: Sew the cord in place, using *pick stitch* (p. 13). 3a Make sure the beginning and end are firmly secured.

Tip: Depending on the type of fabric you are using, you can also do this by machine: simply thread the machine with a matching yarn and stitch along the line, keeping to the center of the cord. 3b This is best done with a special embroidery foot on the appropriate machine settings (see "Machine Embroidery," p. 15).

TIP

Cords are available in various thicknesses and types and should be chosen according to your design and fabric. Velvet cord will add a touch of elegance, for example—and you can create some great effects with homemade cords, too (see "Puma T-shirt," p. 82). Either way, you should wash the cord—as well as the fabric—before you start, so that it doesn't pucker with subsequent washing.

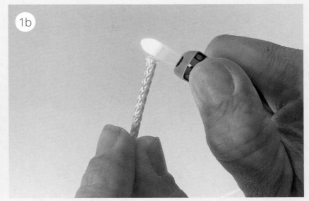

WALL HANGING
Coral

One-line embroidery in its simplest form! Big and bold, this abstract drawing echoes the style of painter Henri Matisse. If you want more-abstract designs, you'll find endless inspiration among the works of expressionist artists.

MATERIALS

- Cotton rug. Used here: 23.5" × 35.5" (60 × 90 cm); can be bought cheaply from large furniture stores.
- Fabric marker (e.g., water-soluble felt tip)
- Coral-colored fabric or acrylic paint
- Flat, thick-bristle paintbrush
- Jersey yarn (e.g., Freya Cheerful in dark gray)
- Darning needle, 2.75" (7 cm)
- Twig (e.g., from a birch tree)
- (Macramé) cord

1. Transfer: Copy the design from the pattern onto paper and cut out. Place the pattern on your rug and pin in place. (When positioning the design, bear in mind that the upper selvedge will need to be folded over at the top later on to accommodate the twig.) Now trace the outline and remove the pattern.

2. Color design: Draw a circle on the rug; ours is 8.5" (22 cm) dia. Color in with fabric paint and leave to dry thoroughly.

3. Embroidery: Embroider the design by using *stem stitch* (p. 12). Start at the lowest point and work your way up, covering one to two rows of the weave at a time. **Tip:** This approach is similar to embroidering knitted fabrics (see "Sweater" instructions, p. 92, step 2).

4. Finishing: Fold over the top edge of the rug and hand-sew the twig in place with twine, using large stitches. Cut the cord to the desired length and fasten to the twig.

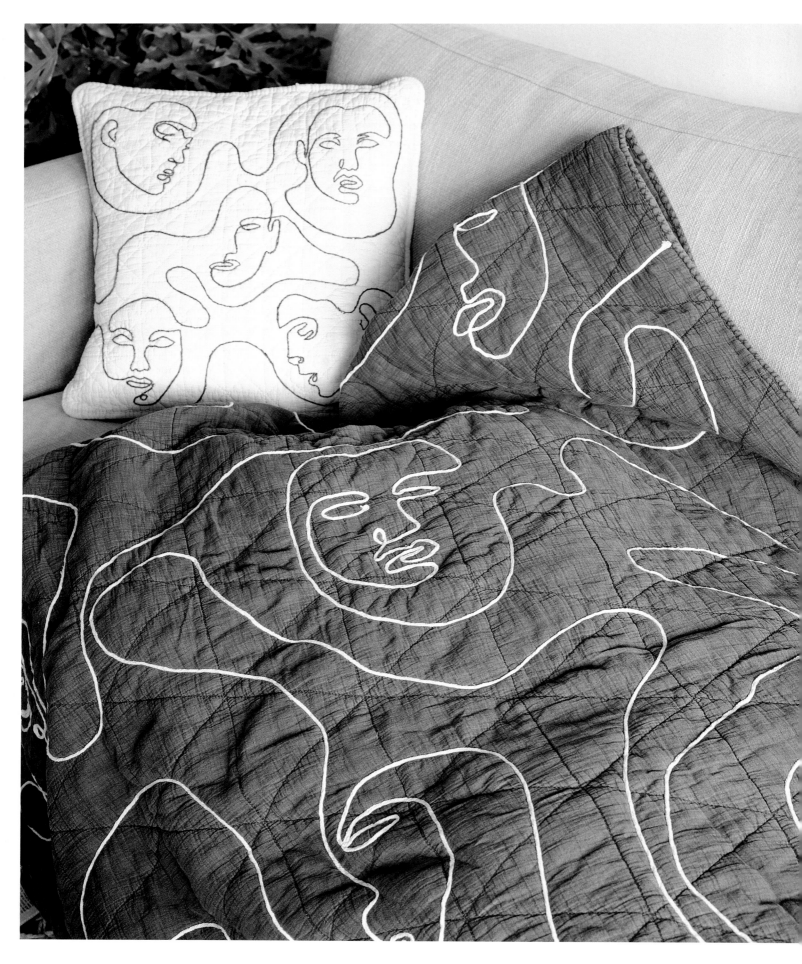

COVERLET *Faces*

MATERIALS

- Plain coverlet
- Suitable transfer medium (e.g., transfer paper)
- Fabric marker (e.g., chalk)
- Reel of cotton cord (e.g., white)
- Fabric glue pen (e.g., Sewline)
- Sewing machine with embroidery foot

Open one-line drawings can be used to create patterns that look fabulous on coverlets and plaids. The designs are simply appliquéd onto the fabric with a cord. On the pattern pages you'll find a selection of designs that you can mix and match as you wish. Alternatively, you can play around with the cord and create your own faces and patterns directly on the fabric—let your imagination run riot! Do make sure the coverlet you are using is not too big and bulky, though, since this will make it relatively hard to machine.

COVERLET

(Illustrated instructions for appliquéing cords can be found on p. 52.)

1. Preparing the pattern: Choose any number of designs from the patterns and enlarge them to the desired format (see "Scaling," p. 8). You'll find the simpler drawings easier to work with later on. Trace each of the faces onto paper any way you like (e.g., as a mirror image). Cut out the patterns roughly and distribute over the coverlet.

2. Transfer: Copy the designs to the cover (e.g., with *transfer paper* [p. 9]). (The lines will be covered by the cord later on.) Now draw in some nice wavy lines between the faces.

3. Laying the cord: Starting at the edge of the coverlet, lay the (prewashed) cord along the lines. Fix in place with the glue pen.

Tip: Some of the one-line faces are open on one side, and others on both sides. This means that not all of them can be joined with a single line. You will therefore need to divide the cord into several sections and lay them separately until the whole pattern is completed and secured. The important thing is to keep the cord flat and not too taut.

4. Appliqué: Stitch the cords in place by machine. For this, it's best to use the embroidery foot with the appropriate settings (see "Machine Embroidery," p. 15). Depending on the size and material of the coverlet, you can also appliqué the cord in the normal way with the standard sewing foot, or by hand using *pick stitch* (p. 13).

MATERIALS

- (Quilted) cushion cover and cushion. Used here: 15.75" × 15.75" (40 × 40 cm).
- Suitable transfer medium (e.g., tear-away stabilizer)
- Fabric marker (e.g., Trick Marker)
- Yarn (e.g., gray embroidery floss)
- Embroidery needle

MORE ALL-OVER PATTERNS . . .

QUILTED CUSHION
Faces

1. Transfer: Trace as many designs as you like from the patterns onto *tear-away stabilizer* (p. 9), cut them out roughly, and position them on the cushion cover. Now draw in some nice wavy lines between the faces (see coverlet instructions).

2. Embroidery: Embroider the lines, using *split stitch* (p. 12) or another line stitch of your choice.

"ROSE" SWEATER

Transfer and embroidery: see
instructions for "Selfie Sweater"
(p. 90)

Fashion

One-line drawings on clothing and accessories are very much in vogue and always look stylish—whether on bags, shirts, or pants.

(See page 95 for the patterns for these projects.)

SWEATSHIRT *Divided*

One-line drawings look great on men's clothing too! This trendy design is a real eye-catcher, and perfect for embroidering in two different colors. The backstitches are deliberately sewn in slightly irregular lengths to create a subtle scribble effect.

MATERIALS

- Plain sweatshirt
- Suitable transfer medium (e.g., transfer paper)
- Embroidery yarn (e.g., white and yellow embroidery floss)
- Embroidery needle

1. Transfer: Copy the design to the sweatshirt (e.g., with *transfer paper* [p. 9]). The best way to do this is to place a hard object (piece of cardboard or chopping board) inside for support. For dark fabrics, *tear-away stabilizer* is also a good alternative.

2. Embroidery: Embroider half the design in white and the other half in yellow, using *backstitch* (p. 11). To change color, follow the same procedure as for weaving in the thread (see "Weaving In & Securing the Thread," p. 10). Remember to keep your backstitches very small on the curves.

PHONE CASE
Girl Power

MATERIALS

- Clear phone case
- Cardstock
- Smooth white cotton fabric
- Double-sided adhesive fusible bonding web
- Suitable transfer medium (e.g., transfer paper)
- Sewing machine with embroidery foot
- Black sewing yarn
- Utility knife

Cell phones are our daily companions and—like handbags—they also make a stylish fashion accessory. With a clear phone case, you can ring in the new whenever you feel like it, simply by inserting your own card-embroidered design. This can be created in no time on the machine, and the smooth, flat stitching means you can slip your phone back in again with ease.

PHONE CASE

1. Prep: Place the phone on the cardstock and draw around the outline (= embroiderable area). Cut out, allowing a margin of approx. 0.75" (2 cm) all the way around. Now cut an identical piece out of the fabric.

2. Transfer: Transfer the design from the pattern to the fabric (e.g., using the *light box method* [p. 9]). Position the design so that the main part is inside the embroiderable area. (Do draw in the lines in the margin as well—this will be trimmed away later.) Now iron the fabric onto the paper, using double-sided adhesive fusible bonding web (see "Tool Kit," p. 8).

3. Embroidery: Machine slowly along the line, using the embroidery foot (see "Machine Embroidery," p. 15).

4. Finishing: Trim off the margin around the edges and insert the card into your phone case embroidered side up. Now draw in the hole for the camera and cut it out carefully with a very sharp utility knife. Finally, pop your phone back in!

MORE GIRL POWER . . .

BLAZER

MATERIALS

- Plain blazer
- Seam ripper
- Suitable transfer medium (e.g., transfer paper)
- Yarn (e.g., cream crochet thread)
- Embroidery needle
- Sewing needle and thread (in same color as blazer)

1. Prep: With lined garments such as blazers, you will need to begin by unpicking a small section of the inside lining where you plan to embroider. Embroidering through both layers of fabric could cause the outer fabric to pucker.

2. Transfer: Copy the design to the blazer (e.g., with *transfer paper* [p. 9]). Take particular care around the darts and keep the fabric taut throughout so as not to distort the design.

3. Embroidery: Thread the needle and secure the end of the thread with a knot. Bring the needle up through the opening in the lining and embroider the design, using *split stitch* (p. 12) or similar. Finally, close the opening again by using *pick stitch* (p. 13).

STRAW BAG *Elephant*

Not only are elephants a trendy design, they are also one of the most intelligent mammals on the planet. This project is a tribute to those majestic gray giants! Embroidering on straw is not generally difficult. Instead of thick wool, you can also use another yarn such as raffia, for example.

MATERIALS

- Plain straw bag. Used here: approx. 19.5" (50 cm) w × 13.75" (35 cm) h.
- Pins
- Tear-away stabilizer
- Thick yarn (e.g., gray wool)
- Large, sharp needle (suitable for yarn)
- Thimble (optional)

1. Transfer: Copy the design onto *tear-away stabilizer* (p. 9) and cut out roughly. Pin the stabilizer onto the bag.

2. Embroidery: *Split stitch* (p. 12) is a good choice for this project. Try not to insert the needle into the straw seams, but always slightly offset. **Tip:** Try to avoid unpicking your stitches, since the thick yarn will leave visible holes!
Once it's complete, remove the stabilizer carefully with the needle.

DENIM JACKET
Koi Fish

It's hard to believe that this artistic drawing—a typically Japanese design—consists of a single line! A distinctive feature here is the use of different stroke thicknesses, rendered by two different types of stitching. Alternatively, you can use yarns of two different types or colors.

MATERIALS

- Denim jacket
- Suitable transfer medium (e.g., transfer paper)
- Fabric marker (e.g., chalk)
- Yarn (e.g., white crochet thread)
- Embroidery needle

1. Transfer: Copy the design to the jacket (e.g., with *transfer paper* [p. 9]). For this, it's best to slip a hard object (e.g., piece of cardboard) underneath for support. Mark the two different stroke thicknesses on the pattern with a fabric marker.

2. Embroidery: Embroider the design by using two different stitches (e.g., a small *split stitch* [p. 12]) for the thin lines and *chain stitch* (p. 13) for the thick ones.

TANK TOP
Beauty in Bloom

MATERIALS

- Plain white tank top
- Water-based fabric paint (e.g., Marabu in pink and blue)
- Small sponge
- Paintbrush
- Suitable transfer medium (e.g., self-adhesive stabilizer)
- Yarn (e.g., gray embroidery floss)
- Embroidery needle

This dreamy face goes well with floral designs, though any other patterns featuring flowers or leaves will look good too. When choosing a jersey top to embroider, you should generally avoid anything too close fitting, since it can result in puckering.

Self-adhesive stabilizer makes an ideal transfer medium; it also stiffens the jersey fabric and does the job of an embroidery hoop by keeping it taut.

TANK TOP

1. Color design: In order to position the color patches to best effect, first slip the pattern together with a hard support (e.g., board) inside the top so that the lines of the drawing show through. Using a small sponge, dampen the areas to be painted, and add just a few drops of paint. Leave to dry thoroughly, then heat-set by ironing without steam for approx. three minutes.

2. Transfer: Transfer the design to the fleecy side of the *self-adhesive stabilizer* (see "Water-Soluble Stabilizer," p. 9) and cut out around it. Now peel off the backing paper and press onto the top.

3. Embroidery: Embroider along the line of the design (e.g., using *split backstitch* [p. 11]) or any other line stitch of your choice. When complete, soak in a bowl of water and remove the stabilizer.

MORE BEAUTY IN BLOOM . . .

VELVET SHOES
Blossoms

1. Transfer: Copy the design onto *tear-away stabilizer* (p. 9) and cut out roughly. Pin the design to the front of the shoe—not too far forward, since this will limit your room for maneuver.

2. Embroidery: Embroidering on velvet is a bit trickier than on smooth woven fabrics, because the stitches tend to "sink" into the deep pile, making it difficult to bring the needle in and out with the required precision. In our experience, the best stitch to use here is *whipped backstitch* (p. 11). Embroider the line of backstitch first, keeping the yarn relatively taut. Then remove the stabilizer with a needle. (Don't worry if the embroidered line doesn't look entirely regular—any blips will be evened out by the whipping thread.)

MATERIALS

- Chinese-style velvet shoes (classic type, available from stores or via the internet)
- Suitable transfer medium (e.g., tear-away stabilizer)
- Yarn (e.g., pink crochet thread)
- Embroidery needle

TIP

When embroidering shoes, always start at the widest part of the toe. The closer you are to the opening of the shoe, the easier it will be to weave in the thread later on.

SUMMER DRESS
Poppies

This scaled-up flower design looks great on simple dresses or skirts. In this case, the design was embroidered by machine, which saves time.

MATERIALS

- Plain dress
- Fusible interfacing (optional)
- Suitable transfer medium
- Sewing yarn (e.g., black)
- Sewing machine with embroidery foot

1. Transfer: If the dress is made of a lightweight fabric, transfer the design by using a *fusible interfacing* (see "Tool Kit," p. 8). To do this, trace the pattern twice (once as a mirror image) onto the interfacing and cut out as close to the designs as you can. Position on the wrong side of the fabric and iron in place. **Tip:** If your fabric doesn't need stiffening, you can also use *tear-away stabilizer* (p. 9) instead.

2. Embroidery: Adjust the machine to the correct settings and, starting on the wrong side of the fabric, stitch along the line of each design once (see "Machine Embroidery," p. 15). Now turn the dress onto the right side and go over the lines again until they stand out clearly.

TOTE BAG
Monstera Leaves

Monstera leaves are in at the moment, gracing fashion and home accessories alike, but their beauty is constant. This versatile drawing can be scaled up or down for use on larger areas or in combination with other one-line drawings (see "Flamingo Soap Bag," p. 34). If you wish, you can also add a color element to the bag before embroidering it (see "A Few More Ideas," p. 94).

MATERIAL

- Plain fabric bag. Used here: approx. 15" (38 cm) w × 16.5" (42 cm) h.
- Suitable transfer medium (e.g., transfer paper)
- Yarn (e.g., black crochet thread)
- Embroidery needle
- Leather straps
- Double-sided adhesive fusible bonding web (optional)
- Sewing machine or needle and thread (in same color as straps)

1. Transfer: Copy the design to the bag (e.g., with *transfer paper* [p. 9]).

2. Embroidery: Embroider along the line of the design, using *split stitch* (p. 12). You can also use any other line stitch instead.

3. Finishing: Cut off the fabric handles of the bag and sew on the leather straps in their place, either by hand or machine. It's a good idea to secure the straps to the bag beforehand with a piece of *double-sided adhesive fusible bonding web* (see "Tool Kit," p. 8) to stop them slipping as you sew.

SWEATSHIRT *Wildcat*

MATERIALS

- Plain sweatshirt
- Suitable transfer medium (e.g., transfer paper)
- Black synthetic cord
- Lighter
- Fabric glue pen
- Black sewing thread
- Sewing needle

This minimalist cat design looks really cool on a sweatshirt! Here, the bold, thick lines can't be embroidered on directly, since a yarn that thick would damage the knit fabric. Instead, the design is appliquéd onto the garment with a cord—a quick and hassle-free method that creates a fabulous effect.

SWEATSHIRT

(Illustrated instructions for appliquéing cords can be found on p. 52.)

1. Transfer: Copy the design to the sweatshirt (e.g., with *transfer paper* [p. 9]). It's best to place a hard object underneath for support (e.g., cutting board or piece of cardboard).

2. Positioning the cord: Singe the end of the cord with a lighter to fuse the fibers together and prevent them from fraying when washed. Now position the cord along the predrawn line and fix in place with the glue pen.

Continue step by step until the whole design is positioned and glued in place. Make sure the cord lies flat and is not too taut. Finally, seal the end of the cord with the lighter.

3. Appliqué: Sew the cord in place, using *pick stitch* (p. 13). Make sure the beginning and end are well secured to stop them coming undone when washed.

MORE WILDCAT APPLIQUÉ IDEAS . . .

T-SHIRT
Puma

MATERIALS

- Plain black T-shirt
- Suitable transfer medium (e.g., transfer paper)
- Thin crochet thread in turquoise
- Suitable crochet needle (approx. 0.05" [1.5 mm])
- Fabric glue pen
- Embroidery needle
- Sewing thread (in same color as crochet thread)
- Sewing needle

1. Transfer: Copy the design to the T-shirt (e.g., with *transfer paper* [p. 9]).

2. Crocheting the cord: Crochet a long cord, using chain stitch. Instead of closing the end, open up the last chain loop to stop the cord from unraveling. You can adjust the exact length of cord later.

3. Positioning the cord: Thread the end of the yarn onto the needle and bring up through the fabric at the starting point of the line. Secure with a knot on the reverse. Now position the cord along the predrawn line and fix in place with the glue pen. Continue step by step in this way, crocheting extra stitches or undoing them as necessary until you reach the end of the line. Then cut off the thread, pull it through the last stitch, and feed the end back through the fabric with the needle. Weave in both ends of the yarn on the reverse.

4. Appliqué: Sew the crocheted cord in place, using *pick stitch* (p. 13).

CLUTCH
Hand lettering

MATERIALS

- Plain (artificial) leather clutch bag. Used here: 11.5" (29 cm) w × 8.5" (22 cm) h.
- Various material remnants (e.g., leather, paper fabric, and washable paper in white, black, and silver)
- Fabric glue
- Suitable transfer medium (e.g., transfer paper)
- Yarn (e.g., embroidery floss in white, black, and silver)
- Embroidery needle

Inspired by the exquisite hand-lettering styles often used in bullet journals, one-line lettering also looks extremely stylish on clothing and accessories. There are special hand-lettering fonts available for this, some of which may need a little manual adjustment to turn them into one-line designs. Another lettering pattern can be found on the pattern pages (see "A Few More Ideas," p. 94).

If you want to replicate your own handwriting, you can produce a pattern by hand or on the computer.

CLUTCH

(Instructions for the DIY version of the bag can be found on p. 34.)

1. Color design: Cut one circle each out of the white leather and black paper fabric; ours is 3.25" (8.5 cm) and 4.75" (12 cm) dia. Arrange the circles on the bag so that they overlap. Trace the shape created by the overlap onto a piece of silver washable paper and cut out. If necessary, attach the three elements to the bag with a little fabric glue or *double-sided adhesive fusible bonding web* (see "Tool Kit," p. 8). Now sew on all the way around, using *backstitch* (p. 11) in the appropriate colors.

2. Transfer: Position the lettering on the bag and transfer (e.g., with *transfer paper* [p. 9]), extending the lines as far as you wish.

3. Embroidery: Embroider the lettering by using *pick stitch* (p. 12). To create the effect of a progressively thinning line, proceed as follows:

Start with six strands from the white embroidery floss and separate them out one by one as you go, so that you end up sewing with just one strand. Finally, weave in the separated strands on the reverse.

MORE HAND LETTERING . . .

T-SHIRT

MATERIALS

- Plain white T-shirt
- Suitable transfer medium (e.g., self-adhesive stabilizer)
- Yarn (e.g., black crochet thread)
- Embroidery needle

1. Transfer: Using transfer paper, trace the design onto the fleecy side of the *self-adhesive stabilizer* (see "Water-Soluble Stabilizer," p. 9) and cut out around it. Then remove the backing paper and glue the design onto the T-shirt.

2. Embroidery: *We* recommend *chain stitch* (p. 13) for lettering. Once it's complete, soak your embroidery in water and remove the stabilizer remnants.

JEANS
Modern Art

Jeans look fabulous with an embroidered design. And you don't have to limit yourself to the classically understated pocket or side seam either: abstract one-line drawings are perfect for making a big splash! If you wish, you can also embroider your jeans with a punch needle—there are lots of good books and online tutorials on this.

MATERIALS
- Plain jeans
- Suitable transfer medium (e.g., transfer paper)
- Embroidery yarn (e.g., white mercerized cotton yarn)

1. Transfer: Copy the designs to the jeans (e.g., with *transfer paper* [p. 9]). For this, it's best to place a hard object (piece of cardboard) inside the leg for support.

2. Embroidery: *Backstitch* (p. 11) lends itself to the look of this design, although any other line stitch will do just as well. When weaving in the thread ends, it helps to turn the jeans onto the wrong side.

SWEATER
Selfie

MATERIALS

- Plain chunky knit sweater
- Fabric marker (e.g., water-soluble felt tip)
- Tear-away stabilizer (optional)
- Tacking thread (optional)
- Thick yarn (e.g., in gray)
- Darning needle (2.75" [7 cm])

Knitted sweaters are another good candidate for embroidery—and the result will look like part of the knit design! This time, why not leave the patterns aside and make up your own? Just grab a long piece of yarn and play around with it: floral patterns, single lines, or faces—wherever your fancy takes you! (For more freehand inspiration, see the espadrilles on page 103.)

SWEATER

1. Positioning the design: Take a long piece of yarn and make your own pattern on the sweater. When you're happy with it, trace the outline with the fabric marker, keeping close to the yarn. 1a Note that fabric markers don't work on all knits; when that's the case, draw the design onto *tear-away stabilizer* (p. 9) and tack along the line, using a simple running stitch, so that you end up with a dotted line. 1b Then carefully remove the stabilizer and embroider along the dotted line as described in step 2. (Remove the tacking).

2. Embroidery: *Stem stitch* (p. 12) is ideal for embroidering chunky knits. The following tips will help keep your work nice and even (for finer knits, just adapt the number of knit stitches accordingly):

First, insert the needle between two knit stitches from the back and pull the thread through to the front. 2

Skip two whole stitches, then insert the needle and bring it up again between the two stitches. 3

Now skip one whole stitch, insert the needle, and bring it up again where you inserted it for your first stem stitch. 4 Be careful not to pull the thread too tight. Continue in the same way.

Tip: If your design has vertical lines, you won't be able to base your spacing on the knit stitch width; in that case, just try to keep your stitches roughly the same length.

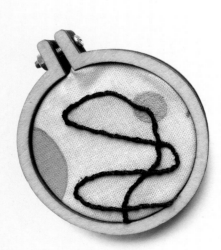

TIP

A great way to show off your freehand embroidery designs is to mount them in mini embroidery hoops and turn them into pendants or key fobs. Whipped backstitch (p. 11) is ideal for miniature one-line drawings. In this example, the fabric was colored with acrylic paint prior to embroidering.

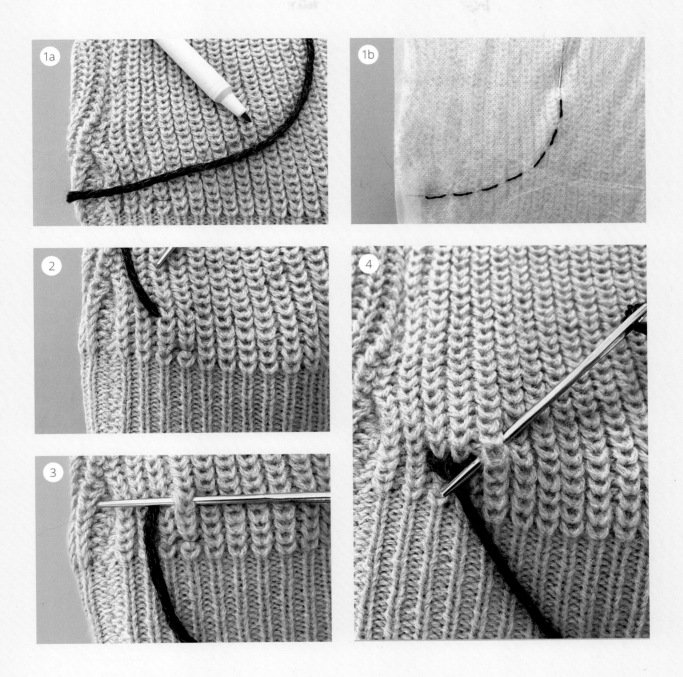

A Few More Ideas

Here's a sneak peek at some more designs generated in the making of this book!

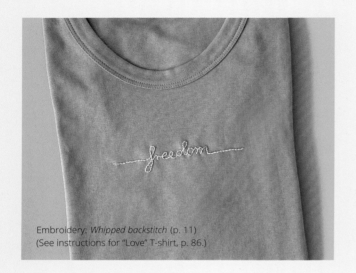

Embroidery: *Whipped backstitch* (p. 11)
(See instructions for "Love" T-shirt, p. 86.)

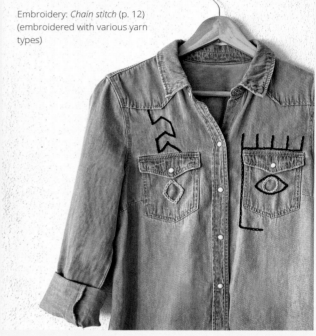

Embroidery: *Chain stitch* (p. 12)
(embroidered with various yarn types)

Color design: Fabric and acrylic paint

Embroidery: *Split stitch* (p. 12)
(See instructions for "Shy Lady" Picture, p. 26.)

Color design: Fabric paint
Embroidery: *Split stitch* (p. 12)

Patterns

Bunny Canvas Basket, p. 44

Eye-Catcher Cushion, p. 50

Hummingbird Dish Towels, p. 46

Naive Art Vase, p. 48

Pattern Layout Diagram

Fabric

Seam allowance (1 cm)

Embroidery

Coral Wall Hanging,
p. 54

Faces Coverlet and Cushion, pp. 56–58

Ginkgo Table Linens, p. 22

Feather Wooden Trinket Box, p. 36

Flamingo Soap Bag, p. 34

Palm Leaf Cosmetic Bag, p. 32

Inspirations Wall Art, p. 94

Eucalyptus Velvet Cushion, p. 18

Panda Cork Picture, p. 20

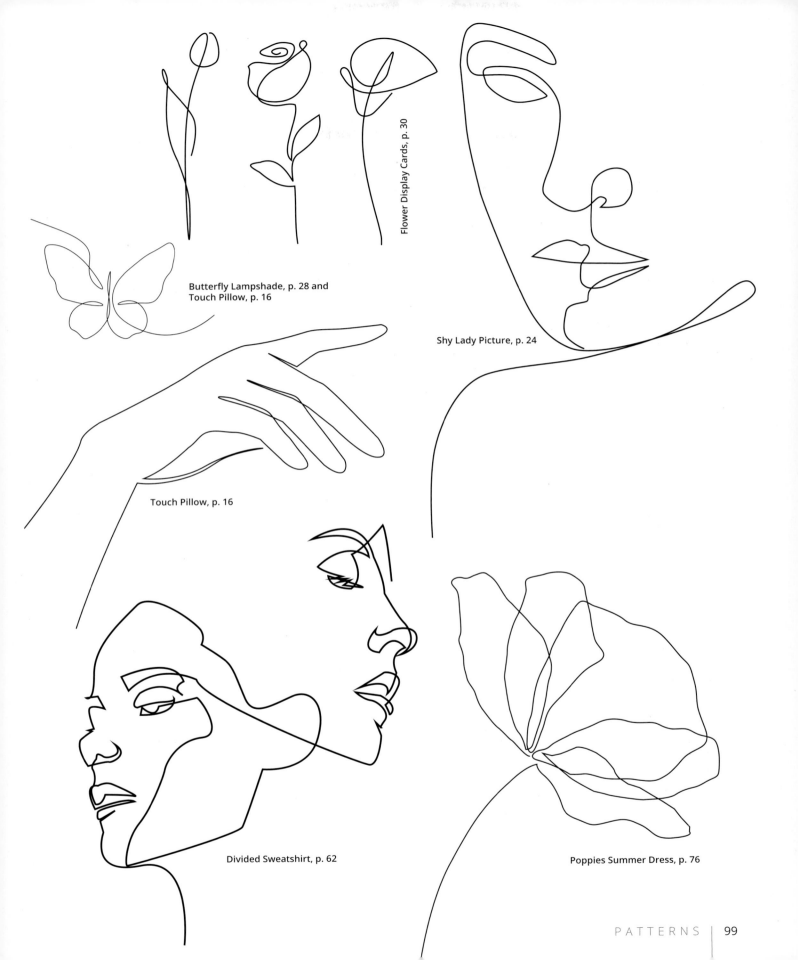

Flower Display Cards, p. 30

Butterfly Lampshade, p. 28 and
Touch Pillow, p. 16

Shy Lady Picture, p. 24

Touch Pillow, p. 16

Divided Sweatshirt, p. 62

Poppies Summer Dress, p. 76

Wildcat Sweatshirt, p. 80

Monstera Leaves Tote Bag, p. 78

Rose Sweater, p. 60

Beauty in Bloom Tank Top, p. 72, and
Blossom Velvet Shoes, p. 74

Foxy Animal Pillow, p. 42

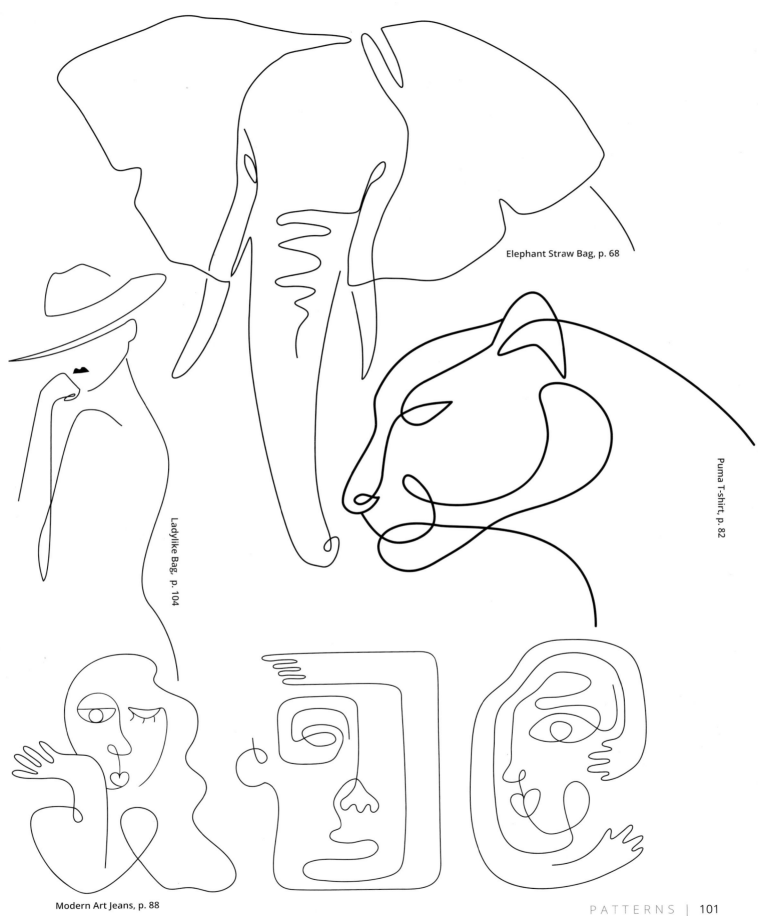

Elephant Straw Bag, p. 68

Puma T-shirt, p. 82

Ladylike Bag, p. 104

Modern Art Jeans, p. 88

Hummingbird Top, p. 14

Girl Power Phone Case, p. 64

Joy Blazer, p. 66

Koi Fish Denim Jacket, p. 70

Girl with a Bun Wall Art, p. 40

Inspirations T-shirt, p. 94

Hand Lettering T-shirt and Clutch, p. 84

A BIG
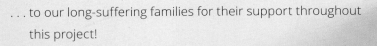
Thank-You . . .

. . . to our long-suffering families for their support throughout this project!

. . . to Mary for creating such delightful one-line drawings for this book

. . . to Elisabeth Berkau for her superb contemporary photography

. . . to our wonderful model Bianca Szabowski, who stepped in at short notice to give our fashion photos a touch of star quality!

. . . to our proofreader Johanna Heiß for her eagle eye and her support and motivation

Embroidery: *Split stitch* (p. 12)
(See tip below instructions for
"Blossom" Velvet Shoes, p. 75.)

"LADYLIKE" BAG

Transfer medium: *Transfer paper* (p. 9)
Line drawing: *Split stitch* (p. 12)
Mouth: *Backstitch* (p. 11)